TABLE OF CONTENTS

Workbook Answers

Reading: Literature

The Big Picture Answers

Mom's Big Idea

1. Janey's mom says cars and trucks are "flying down the road." She means they are going at high rates of speed.
2. Janey
3. c
4. We learn that she has tried many times to get something done about the problem of speeding vehicles, but no one at City Hall will do anything about it.
5. b
6. She is afraid that someone is going to get hit by a car or truck.
7. "Don't keep us in the dark" is the figurative phrase. He means that Janey's mom shouldn't keep her idea a secret from them.
8. d
9. b
10. Answers will vary.

Mom Makes a List

1. c
2. Janey
3. a
4. She uses the phrase "all your ducks in a row", which means to be organized and ready to go
5. Answers will vary.
6. mil | lion   do | main   tech | nic | al   host | ing
7. b
8. "Boy oh boy, there's a lot more to making a website than I thought there was."
"I couldn't figure that stuff out in a million years."

9. A dictionary
10. Answers will vary

Mom Launches Her Website
1. She would be unhappy, because she likes sleeping in and having late breakfasts on Saturdays.
2. It means she couldn't figure out exactly what was different. People use this expression when they know something is wrong, or different, but don't know exactly what is wrong or different.
3. d
4. He winked because he was joking; he didn't really think Janey was going to reprimand her mom.
5. A "night owl" is someone who likes to stay up very, very late.
6. c
7. Janey's mom
8. a
9. Answers will vary.
10. Answers will vary.

Lights! Camera! Janey!
1. c
2. Janey's mom
3. dangerous/unsafe/risky
4. b
5. All Janey could think about was getting home to make the video, so she was bored with school.
6. d
7. Because she memorized her script right away, and then practiced her lines every day.
8. a
9. Answers will vary.
10. c

A Team Effort

1. c
2. effect   cause
3. Answers will vary.
4. activity   congratulate
5. d
6. Answers will vary.
7. persuade
8. She means it's something she enjoys a lot.
9. congratulate
10. The friends and neighbors who called and wrote to City Hall about the speeding problem.

The Big Picture Quiz Answers

1. Chapter 4
2. any three of these: riding her bike, Saturdays, going to school, eating pancakes, eating pizza
3. Chapter 3
4. Chapter 5
5. pancakes and pizza
6. She had called, emailed, and visited City Hall
7. Answers will vary.
8. Answers will vary.
9. Old Mill Road
10. Answers will vary.

How Nian Was Defeated answers

1. ocean
2. No; it's a folk tale, and folk tales aren't true. And there are no monsters who come out of the ocean once a year and eat people.
3. China. We can assume it's China because we're told it's a Chinese folk tale, and it's the explanation for the ways people in China celebrate New Year's Day.
4. He was smiling mysteriously because he knew the secret of how to defeat Nian, so he wasn't scared.

5. shaking or trembling

6. Peach Blossom. We know this because Peach Blossom appears in parentheses right after the word Taohun. This is the author's way of telling us what Taohun means in English.

7. great fear, terror

8. Even though the story isn't true, it still has a central lesson or point. The central lesson of the story is how the customs of Chinese New Year's celebrations came about.

9. c –This story is a myth and so is *The Legend of Paul Bunyan*, while all the other books contain true stories.

10. Answers can vary, but most likely the old beggar had no trouble getting food in the future because the villagers regarded him as a hero because he had defeated the monster that had terrorized them for years.

Reading: Informational Texts

Our Neighbor Mercury Answers
1. Mercury is the tiny planet closest to the sun.
2. b
3. The temperatures are too harsh.
4. Earth
5. b
6. d
7. a
8. craters
9. c
10. Answers will vary.
11. It means very old, or a long time ago. The sentence tells us that Mercury was named 24 centuries ago, which is the clue a person can use to figure out the meaning of *ancient*.
12. orbit
13. Because Mercury is much closer to the sun
14. Because it is one of the planets closest to Earth. The author is using the word in a figurative way.
15. Not really. A neighbor is someone or something that's near another. Because outer space is so huge, 40 million miles is a small distance compared to the distance from Earth to many other objects in space. But a person who lives 40 miles away would not be close to you at all.

Montana: Big Sky Country Answers
1. border
2. extremely large
3. c
4. d
5. In the western part of the state
6. Yellowstone National Park
7. The US Army
8. a
9. legendary

10. a
11. a verb
12. Answers will vary

Linda Richards, Medical Pioneer Answers
1. b
2. d
3. c
4. century
5. a
6. No; she was born in 1841, and home computers weren't around before about 1980.
7. b
8. c
9. a = 4   b = 1   c = 3   d = 2
10. improve

Becoming a Teacher Answers
1. b
2. b
3. No
4. *Just realize that becoming a teacher is not a piece of cake!*
5. He means it's not easy.

Polar Bears Answers
1. No; polar bears are only found in Norway, Greenland, Russia, Canada, and Alaska.
2. b
3. *Ursus maritimus*
4. They went extinct
5. They have a lot of fur to keep them warm | their fur is white so they blend in and can sneak up on seals for food | they have big feet and big claws so they don't slide on the ice | they have long necks and snouts so they can reach under the ice to look for food
6. No; he is brown, and he doesn't live near the North Pole.

7. Yes; polar bear cubs stay with their mothers for around two years.

8. To accomplish a goal; to achieve what one sets out to do

Walrus Answers

1. The sentence that talks about them using their tusks to move across the ice.

2. An opinion. Some people might find them funny looking, but others might not.

3. Extremely big

4. The sentences that come just before – they are talking about the fact that walruses are very big: *Walruses are also huge. They are between eight and twelve feet long, and can weigh nearly 4,000 pounds.*

5. In a dictionary

6. A verb

7. *get older*

8. An animal that kills and eats another animal

9. Taking the entire sentence together gives a clue: *There aren't many animals that eat walruses, which is a good thing, because they are so big they can't move fast enough to get away from a predator.* It's about animals that eat walruses.

10. Its whiskers

Levi Coffin: President of the Underground Railroad Answers

1. No, he grew up in a Quaker family, and Quakers disapproved of slavery.

2. Fact

3. Because he hated slavery, and slavery was illegal there.

4. No; the story says that if slaves got to Canada they would be free.

5. d

6. Fugitive

7. illegal

8. legal and –il

9. a = 2   b = 4   c = 1   d = 3

10. Newport

One Giant Leap for Mankind Answers

1. In 1961
2. Because no one had ever done it before (or) Because it had seemed impossible for centuries
3. He was a fighter pilot for the Navy
4. brave
5. c
6. A small town. We know this because the article says Neil Armstrong is from there, and it also calls him *the man from a small Ohio town.*
7. *out of the spotlight*
8. Neil Armstrong was "out of this world" when he flew to the moon. Also, "out of this world" is a figure of speech meaning very special, or extraordinary, and Neil Armstrong lived an extraordinary life.

Reading: Foundational Skills

Prefixes Answers

1. d
2. c
3. a
4. b
5. c
6. c
7. a
8. b
9. b
10. d
11. a
12. b
13. d
14. c
15. a

Suffixes answers

1. d
2. a
3. c
4. c
5. b
6. d
7. a
8. c
9. b
10. d

Understanding Latin Suffixes Answers

1. kings, queens, princes and princesses = royalty
2. money given to someone for doing something = payment
3. scare the daylights out of = terrify

4. having nothing to eat for a long time = starvation
5. lights and appliances are powered by this = electricity
6 a big party = celebration
7 able to be bent = bendable
8 swear to tell the truth = testify
9 worthy of being looked up to = admirable
10 able to be divided = divisible

Multisyllable Words Answers
1. bowl/ing
2. play/ground
3. bas/ket/ball
4. soc/cer
5. ref/er/ee
6. gym/nast
7.goal/post
8. catch/er
9. out/field/er
10. base/ball
11. quar/ter/back
12. o/ver/time
13. vol/ley/ball
14. um/pire
15. win/ner
16. tack/le
17. score/board
18. fum/ble
19. strike/out
20. ho/mer

Spelling Irregular Words Answers

1. c: friend
2. c: mother
3. c: would
4. a: humor
5. d: busy
6. d: height
7. a: weight
8. b: straight
9. b: Wednesday
10. b: been
11. c: kind
12. a: tissue
13. d: women
14. b: sugar
15. d: laugh
16. d: doubt
17. b: bought
18. a: business
19. d: lose
20. a: could

Language

Do You Know the Parts of Speech? Answers
1. adjectives
2. nouns
3. verbs
4. adverbs
5. pronouns

Plural Nouns Answers
1. tornadoes
2. feet
3. fish
4. elves
5. tomatoes
6. men
7. calves
8. wives
9. towns
10. mice

Abstract Nouns Answers
1. Saturday
2. attitude
3. duty
4. championship
5. appointment
6. math
7. habits
8. allegiance
9. year
10. time

Concrete or Abstract? Answers

1. A
2. C
3. C
4. A
5. A
6. C
7. A
8. C
9. C
10. A

Fun With Irregular Verbs Answers

1. bought
2. kept
3. hung
4. knew
5. met
6. put
7. went
8. lost
9. brought
10. drank

What's Missing? Answers

1. will taste
2. ran
3. will have
4. will kick
5. talk
6. flew
7. slept
8. will speak
9. wake
10. thought

Subject/Verb Agreement Answers

1. teach
2. knows
3. meows
4. sings
5. gallop
6. drink
7. ring
8. hold
9. reads
10. cuts

Match Those Subjects and Verbs! Answers

1. imagine – R
2. are – W (is)
3. drive – R
4. travels – R
5. Think – R
6. takes – W (take)
7. goes – W (go)
8. does –W (do)
9. depend – W (depends)
10. makes – W (make)

Keep Those Pronouns Straight! Answers

1. my
2. their
3. her
4. my
5. us
6. mine
7. her
8. his
9. its
10. they

Pick That Pronoun! Answers

1. Gabrielle   she
2. belongs to him   his
3. Uncle Bob and Aunt Sally   they
4. Fred   he
5. belongs to you and me   ours
6. belongs to me   my
7. you and me   us
8. belongs to the team   theirs
9. belongs to her   hers
10. the toy

Pick the Right Adjective Answers

1. messier
2. friendliest
3. tallest
4. worst
5. heavier
6. more athletic
7. saddest
8. longer
9. roughest
10. bigger

Fill in the Adverb Answers

1. most quickly
2. more loudly (or louder)
3. better
4. more promptly
5. harder
6. slower (or more slowly)
7. most rapidly
8. earlier
9. soonest
10. more neatly

Compound or Complex? Answers

1. compound
2. complex
3. complex
4. compound
5. complex
6. complex
7. complex
8. compound
9. compound
10. complex

Make Your Own Compound Sentences Answers

1. Fred has the flu, and Carol has a cold.
2. I like baseball, but I don't like basketball.
3. You can eat lunch now, or you can eat lunch later.
4. You should study hard so you can pass your test.
5. We read about art museums, and our teacher told us about famous painters.

Make Your Own Complex Sentences Answers

For each problem, either of the answers shown is correct.
1. When the bell rings, it's time for lunch. | It's time for lunch when the bell rings.
2. If you're not feeling well, you should stay home. | You should stay home if you're not feeling well.
3. Unless you eat your vegetables, you won't get dessert. | You won't get dessert unless you eat your vegetables.
4. You must clean your room before you may go outside and play. | Before you may go outside and play, you must clean your room.
5. Watch out for traffic while you ride your bike. | While you ride your bike, watch out for traffic.

Fix Those Titles! Answers

1. Why You Should Exercise Daily
2. Now They Tell Me!
3. North to Alaska
4. The Hound of the Baskervilles
5. A Tale of Two Cities
6. Please Don't Eat the Daisies
7. Indiana Jones and the Last Crusade
8. Uncle Tom's Cabin
9. The Night Before Christmas
10. Willy Wonka and the Chocolate Factory

Commas and Quotations Answers

1. Boise, Idaho
2. "Mom doesn't want us to have snacks before supper," Billy reminded Joanie.
3. Frieda asked, "What time does the bus usually get here?"
4. "Sir," Pedro exclaimed, "you dropped your wallet!" (Or "Sir," Pedro exclaimed, "you dropped your wallet.")
5. Paris, France
6. "Are those your sunglasses?" Molly asked
7. "James and Kirk," said Mr. Brown, "you need to see me after class."
8. Des Moines, Iowa
9. Dad said, "Let's go to the beach this Saturday."
10. "I don't think that's a very good idea, Mabel," her mother replied.

It's Raining Cats and Possessives! Answers

1. Let's say hello to Tanequa's mom.
2. This is Jack's uniform.
3. I rode Freddy's new bike.
4. Here's the baby's bib.
5. The horse's stall needs cleaned.
6. Here's your book.
7. This is Charles's new video game.
8. Your bus is coming.

9. The dog wagged its tail.
10. The boys' fingers were freezing after they built the snowman.

Scrambled Words & Toast Answers

1. impossible
2. probably
3. everybody
4. weather
5. beautiful
6. prettiest
7. laughed
8. question
9. because
10. discover

Base Words and Suffixes Answers

1. scary
2. exciting
3. interesting
4. replacement
5. newest
6. hopeless
7. muddy
8. accidental
9. happiness
10. musicians

What's the Good Word? Answers

1. c
2. a
3. b
4. c
5. b
6. c
7. b
8. c
9. a
10. a

Spoken or Written? Answers

1. S
2. W
3. W
4. S
5. S
6. S
7. W
8. W
9. S
10. W

What Does It Mean? Answers

1. c
2. b
3. a
4. c
5. c
6. a
7. b
8. a
9. b
10. c

Make a New Word Answers
1. disagree
2. unbelievable
3. happiness
4. redo
5. impolite
6. quickly
7. awareness
8. teacher
9. magical
10. cautious

Practice Test Answers

Practice Test #1

Answers and Explanations

1. C: The first paragraph mostly describes Miguel's behavior and actions as a five-year-old during walks with his father. "...he liked to pick up branches and hit them against the ground and the trees. Sometimes he would waive the stick and pretend he was fighting a great battle."

2. D: Miguel showed more interest in the woods by asking his father questions about different trees and plants. As a result of his interest, Miguel learned how to identify trees by their bark and leaves and how trees reproduce by spreading their seeds to other parts of the forest.

3. C: In this paragraph, the word identify is used to show the action of recognizing, or identifying by sight, different trees and plants by the appearance of their bark or leaves. It is different from understanding well because Miguel doesn't have to understand trees very well to identify their leaves and bark.

4. A: This story takes place in a forest. Several hints in the story indicate its location, including mention of taking walks in the woods. Woods is another word for forest. Also, orchards tend to have the same kinds of trees, and gardens and parks tend to be tended neatly without rotting logs lying around.

5. B: Miguel is confused because he did not think of the rotten log as being useful for anyone or anything. He kicked the log for this reason. The news that it served as a home for different insects did not match his impression that rotten logs just take up space and make walking on trails difficult. He

- 24 -

was angry when he almost tripped over the log, but he did not stay angry for long. He was neither happy nor sad.

6. C: The title is located in straight black letters below the name of the publication, Miguel's World. The words "By Martha Gold" in the heading tell who wrote the article.

7. C: In paragraph 6, Miguel's father tells him that the birds are waiting on them to leave so that they can eat.

8. A: In the story, Miguel's father tells him not to kick the log after we learned that he used to play with sticks when he was younger and before Miguel and his father leave the log and Miguel returns to replace the bark and leaves they brushed aside.

9. B: Miguel's father points out how Miguel's attitude toward the log changes. Usually, people love things that they want to protect. Hating something is usually the opposite of wanting to protect it.

10. D: Miguel already was interested in the plants and animals in the woods. Now that he has learned what lives inside old logs, he probably will look for them the next time he comes across an old log lying on the ground.

11. B: The only thing that you can really gather from the picture is that they are talking while walking through the woods. The other answers don't really make sense because Miguel is not holding a stick, and there is no log in the picture.

12. Part A: B: The sentence after the one with the word dart starts with the phrase "it moved so fast." The phrase "it moved so fast" relates to the previous verb, dart.

Part B: C: Based on the answer of "it moved so fast" in Part A, it can be assumed that "dart" means a quick movement.

13. C: The animal moved so quickly that at first, Tanya only could see the animals' colors and not its shape. Maize was a puppy at the time and about the size of a fully-grown skunk, which happens to be black and white.

14. D: Tanya promised her mother that she would take care of Maize. As part of that promise, Tanya had to be home every day to help feed and take care of her dog. Tanya could not go over to her friends' houses after school. After a while Tanya began to miss seeing her friends outside of school.

15. A: Laticia helped solve Tanya's problem by inviting herself over to Tanya's house. This way, Tanya could see her friends and take care of her dog at the same time.

16. A: This title best summarizes the story's main idea that Maize started to look like a burden, but turned out to be a great friend by helping Tanya keep up with her friends after school. The other titles either are inaccurate (Maize is not crazy) or focused too narrowly on one aspect of the story.

17. I, III, V: In the story Tanya's mom states, "You have to feed her, take her out for walks, and train her to behave."

18. B: The story lists the things different kinds of bats eat, including mice, blood, fish and insects.

19. B: Bats live everywhere where there are plants. For that reason, the only places you will not find bats are Antarctica and the North Pole, since those areas are too cold for plants.

20. I, IV: The ways that they help people are discussed in the last paragraph. Some of the other answer choices are discussed in the story, but are not mentioned as ways that bats help people.

21. D: In the story it is stated that, "They are the only mammals that fly."

22. D: The space in the middle of a Venn diagram lists the components that the two sides of the diagram have in common. Both kinds of bats only come out at night.

23. A: The title is the straight, solid name under the name of the publication. It is specific to the article, whereas "Animal Times" is more general and refers to the title of the publication, not the article.

24. C: In the first paragraph it states that "Most bats in North America eat insects that they catch in the air with their teeth." The story does not say anything about bats that come out in daytime, and the other traits belong to different species of bats.

25. C: This choice best summarizes the main idea of the poem, which is about a child at first adoring a toy, but eventually outgrowing it. Like lots of children, she stopped playing with the toy, but kept it for the memories and out of affection for the toy.

26. A: In the first line the author says she was three when she first got the bear.

27. B: The author took the bear everywhere with her when she first got it as a present.

28. B: "His fur wore off in patches" shows how the girl's constant handling wore the bear out.

29. D: "But now I'm too old for teddy bears, so in my room he'll stay" shows that while the author still loves the bear, she now keeps him in her room instead of taking him with her.

30. C: In this poem, the rhyming words are at the end of every two lines.

Part B: C: The words "looks" and "crooks" both end in "ooks", which means they make the same ending sound and rhyme.

31. A: The correct order of events in this poem is: Child receives Sam. Child takes Sam everywhere. Child puts Sam on a shelf.

32. B: While one can eat food cooked by a fire in any of those places, the presence of a picnic table, old trees (where Jake collected kindling) and the grill indicate that they were at a campsite. Additionally, the passage made no mention of water, so it was not by a river or lake.

33. A: By wrapping his finger and thumb in a circle shape around the branches, Jake illustrated the concept of circumference, which is the measure around a circle.

34. The kindling that Jake collected was pronounced good by his father because it was old, dry, brown, and not rotten. Any three of these four would be acceptable answers.

35. D: A fire needs fuel, oxygen, and kindling heat to burn. Food is another name for fuel, and fire specifically needs oxygen.

36. D: In the story Jake gets wood first, then his father starts the fire, and finally Jake gets out hot dogs to cook on the fire.

37. C: The story states specifically that the kindling temperature for wood is 500°F.

38. C: The small circle symbol after the number ° is read as "degrees." The number, the symbol, and the letter after it together are the temperature. Hot and cold are indicated by specific temperatures, not by symbols in the temperature.

39. A: If the iron grill were flammable, it would have burned up along with the wood, leaving Jake and his father without anything on which to cook the hot dogs. This is why they would have ordered pizza for dinner if iron were flammable.

40. D: After this experience, Jake will know to bring wood (fuel), matches (which provide the kindling temperature to start the fire), and paper (which has a lower kindling temperature than wood and is often used to start fires). Jake doesn't need to bring oxygen, since it is readily available.

Practice Test #2

Answers and Explanations

1. A: "Snacks Made Easy" is the title of the story. "Cheese Crackers" is the name of the recipe, and "By Martha Gold" tells who wrote the story.

2. In the recipe under 8 ounces grated cheese it says Cheddar or Monterey Jack.

3. D: Mika said she wanted something NOW because she was hungry, and she wanted something to eat right away. She did not want to wait for the crackers to bake.

4. B: The items needed to make the crackers are listed under the word "ingredients." Therefore, "ingredients" means the items necessary to make a food or dish.

5. Part A: B: Butter is needed in step 2.

Part B: Butter is also needed in step 4.

6. A: By saying to add the water "one tablespoon at a time," the writer is telling the cook to add the water a little bit at a time or gradually.

7. C: The writer listed the steps for making the cheese crackers in numerical order to show the importance of doing things in order when cooking.

8. A: Mika reads the cheese cracker recipe because she wants to make cheese crackers.

9. C: Now that she knows how to make cheese crackers, and she sees that they are easy to make, Mika probably will want to make them again with her mother.

10. A: Gerard, Hakeem's brother, warned him about the old war uniforms room where he heard strange noises and thought he saw a mannequin's eyes move.

11. Part A: D: That's just Sammy's imagination getting out of hand. This phrase tells the reader that Hakeem's mother thinks Sammy makes up things, and she does not trust his judgment.

Part B: B: Mr. Orwell also says that, "Sammy's got a great imagination."

12. C: Hakeem is not afraid of scary movies, and he laughed when he heard ghost stories by a campfire. This shows that Hakeem is brave and does not get scared easily.

13. B: Hakeem believes Gerard because his brother "does not joke around." Also, Hakeem did not think Gerard was trying to scare him, but rather was trying to warn him. This shows that Gerard is honest.

14. C: The flickering overhead light made the shadows around the mannequin's eyes jump. This made the eyes look like they were moving.

15. A: The small number of lamps and the one flickering bulb overhead gave the idea that the room was not lit well. Because of this, the word dim most likely means "badly lit."

16. D: Hakeem laughed because he found out that what his brother thought were ghosts actually were just creaking floorboards and a flickering bulb. He laughed because there was a logical explanation for the scary parts of the room.

17. B: Appearances can be deceiving. The creaking floorboards and jumping shadows mislead Gerard to think a ghost was in the room. What Gerard thought he saw turned out to be something completely different and safe.

18. C: In paragraph 5, the story states, "Ten life-size dummies, or mannequins, each one wearing a different war uniform, stood in the dim room."

19. B: Gloria shows goats, is 12-years-old, and lives on her family farm near Austin, Texas.

20. A: The Texas State Fair is held near Dallas.

21. D: Gloria's family makes cheese from the milk, and they make yarn from the wool produced on their farm.

22. Part A: D: Gloria has five goats. She was only showing two of them at the fair.

Part B: A: She only brought Henry and Maja to show.

23. A: The goats are judged by their appearance (coat, weight, proportions of face and body) and their ability to obey their owner in the show ring.

24. C: After Manuela's father put coffee in his thermos and before they saw Gloria show her goats, Manuela and her father waited for half-an-hour to park.

25. A: The story says that she got into the fair at almost 8 a.m., which is two hours after 6 a.m.

26. C: Right after she talks about them being well fed but not too fat she says, "No ribs showing and no belly sticking out".

27. B: Henry was quiet and did not bleat like Maja. Manuela thought he would win a prize because of his good behavior.

28. D: The squeaky wheel in this story was Maja. Even though she was noisy in the ring, she still won a prize. Perhaps the judges indeed understood "goat"!

29. D: Patricio Suarez is having the party.

30. B: The address for the party, 1234 Main Street, El Paso, is beside the word "where."

31. A: The day and time of the party, which is 2 p.m., is next to "when."

32. D: The invitation says that Patricio is having a birthday party.

33. B: The invitation says reply and then leaves a phone number and an email address.

34. C: Next to "bring," the invitation says "bathing suit." From this, one can infer that swimming will be the main activity at the party.

35. D: Sniffles, sneezing, coughing, and a red nose are all symptoms of a cold.

36. B: The mother tucks her into bed.

37. C: The medicine is purple and thick and tastes like grapes.

38. A: The author likes having her mother's full attention when she is sick.

39. D: The last word in every other line rhymes. So line 1 and 3 rhyme, 2 and 4 rhyme, and so on.

40. B: The story poem starts by saying "At least once a year".

Additional Bonus Material

Due to our efforts to try to keep this book to a manageable length, we've created a link that will give you access to all of your additional bonus material.

Please visit http://www.mometrix.com/bonus948/fsag3elawb to access the information.